ᐅᐱᐅᖅᑕᖅᖁᐅᑦ ᖃᐅᔨᒪᔭᕆᐊᖃᓐᓂᖅ ᐃᓕᓐᓂᐊᕐᓗᒋᑦ!

UUMAJUT

LEARN ABOUT ARCTIC WILDLIFE!

INHABIT MEDIA

IQALUIT • TORONTO

ᐅᑭᐅᖅᑕᖅᑑᑉ ᐆᒪᔪᖏᓐᓂᒃ ᐃᓕᑦᑎᓗᓯ!

UUMAJUT

LEARN ABOUT ARCTIC WILDLIFE!

ᐋᖅᑭᓯᐊᓂᔩᒃ | Edited by

ᓃᓪ ᑯᕆᔅᑕᕗᕐ | Neil Christopher

ᓗᐃᔅ ᕝᓚᕼᐅᕐᑎ | Louise Flaherty

ᑎᑎᕋᖅᑐᖃᓃᑦ | Written by

ᓴᐃᒪᓐ ᐊᕙ | Simon Awa

ᐋᓇ ᓯᒡᓗᕐ | Anna Ziegler

ᔅᑎᐊᕙᓂ ᒪᒃᑖᓄᓪᑦ | Stephanie McDonald

ᐃᓄᒃᑎᑑᓕᖅᑎᑕᖕᒋᑦ | Translated by

ᓕᐊ ᐅᑕᒃ | Leah Otak

ᑎᑎᖅᑐᒐᖅᑕᖕᒋᑦ | Illustrated by

ᕉᒥ ᑲᐃᕋᓐ | Romi Caron

Published by Inhabit Media Inc.
www.inhabitmedia.com

Toronto Office -146A Orchard View Blvd., Toronto, Ontario, M4R 1C3
Iqaluit Office - P.O. Box 11125, Iqaluit, Nunavut, X0A 1H0

Printed and bound in Canada

10 9 8 7 6 5 4 3 2 1

This book has been published with support from the Qikiqtani Inuit Association, Canada Council for the Arts, Nunavut Bilingual Education Society, the Government of Nunavut - Department of Environment, Nunavut Arctic College, and the Rotary Club of Scarborough North.

Canada Council for the Arts | Conseil des Arts du Canada

Qikiqtani Inuit Association

Nunavut
Department of Environment
Havakviat Avatiliqiyikkut
Ministère de l'Environnement

NBES
Nunavut Bilingual Education Society

Rotary International

Nunavut Arctic College

IPY·API
International Polar Year
Année polaire internationale
2007·2008

ᖅᑯᔪᓐᖓᒥᒃᑐᓕᔭᕗᑦ ᐅᖅᑲᑎᒦᒃᔅᒥᖓ Ċᑯᠵᒐᖖᑯ ᐱᓐᒍᖅᑎᑦᑎᖅᑲᑕᐅᔪᓐᐊᓇᑐᐅᒐᒪᒍ ᓴᕆᓇ Ċᑯᠵᐊᑦ,
ᐊᓇᔅ ᠵᓄ, ᓕᐅᐱᓇ ᓄᑯᓕᐊ, ᓚᓐᑦ ᒥᑐᑦᑕᓐ-ᖅᑯᠵᖅᖄ ᐊᒻᒪ ᠵᓗᒍ ᐊᖅᑭᐊᖄᖅ.

We thank Sharina Dodsworth, Anisa Suno, Leeveena Nuyalia, Linda Milton-Kyak, and Seeglook Akeeagok for their contributions.

ᐃᓗᓕᖏᑦ | Contents

ᑕᑯᑎᑦᑎᒋᐊᙵᕐᓂᖅ | Introduction 1

ᓇᑎᕐᓇᐅᑉ ᐆᒪᔪᖏᑦ | Animals of the Tundra.............................. 5

ᐊᕕᙵᖅ | Lemming 7

ᑐᒃᑐ ᐊᖏᓂᖅᓴᖅ | Barren-ground Caribou.............................. 9

ᑐᒃᑐ | Peary Caribou 11

ᑎᕆᒐᓂᐊᖅ ᐅᑭᐅᖅᑕᖅᑐᒥ | Arctic Fox.............................. 13

ᖃᕝᕕᒑᖅᔪᒃ | Wolverine 15

ᑕᓂᐅᕐ ᐱᒍᑕᓗ ᐅᒪᕐᓈᑎᑦ | **Animals of the Sea and Ice** **17**

ᑭᖕᒍᐃᑦ | Amphipods 19

ᐃᖅᑲᓗᒃ ᑕᓂᐅᕐᒥᐅᑕᖅ | Arctic Char 21

ᐅᒡᔪᒃ | Bearded Seal 23

ᖅᐸᓗᒐᖅ | Beluga.. 25

ᐊᕐᕕᖅ | Bowhead Whale 27

ᑐᓂᓯᔪᑦ | **Contributors** **28**

ᑕᑯᑎᑦᑎᒋᐊᙵᕐᓂᖅ | Introduction

ᓄᓇᕗᒻᒥᐅᓄᑦ, ᐃᓅᓯᑦᑎᓐᓄᑦ ᐆᒪᔪᑦ ᐱᒻᒪᕆᐊᓘᒻᒪᑕ. ᐊᖏᔫᑉᐸᑦ ᒥᑭᒃᑲᓗᐊᖅᐸᑕᓗ, ᐊᔾᔨᒌᖕᒋᑦᑐᐊᓘᒻᒪᑕ ᐃᓕᖅᑯᓯᖕᒋᑦ ᖃᐅᔨᔭᐅᑦᑎᑐᐃᓐᓇᖅᑐᑦ. ᓄᓇᕗᒻᒥ ᐆᒪᔪᓕᒫᑦ ᐊᓐᓇᐅᒪᔾᔪᓯᖃᒻᒪᑕ ᐊᔾᔨᒌᖕᒋᑦᑐᓂᒃ ᐅᑭᐅᖅᑕᖅᑐᒥ ᐆᒪᕕᒋᓴᖓᓐᓂ ᐊᖏᕐᕋᓇᓴᑦᑎᓂ.

ᒥᑭᓐᓂᓕᒫᓐᓂ ᐆᒪᔪᕐᓂ ᐃᓕᑉᐸᓪᓚᐊᖏᓐᓇᖅᓯᒪᒐᒪ ᐅᓪᓗᒥ ᓱᓕ ᐃᓕᑉᐸᓪᓚᐊᔪᖓ. ᐅᕙᓐᓄᑦ, ᖃᐅᔨᔪᒪᓪᓚᓇᖅᑲᑦᑕᕋᒪ ᐆᒪᔪᐃᑦ ᐊᑐᖅᑕᐅᖅᑲᑦᑕᕈᓯᕙᓂᖏᓐᓂᒃ ᐃᓄᖕᓄᑦ, ᐃᓕᖅᑯᓯᖏᓪᓗ ᐊᓯᔾᔨᓲᖑᓂᖏᑦ ᓯᓚ ᒪᓕᒃᑐᒍ, ᓯᓚᐅᓪᓗ ᐊᓯᔾᔨᕐᓂᖓᓄᑦ ᐊᑦᑐᖅᑕᐅᓂᖏᑦ,

For people in Nunavut, wildlife plays a very important role. Large and small animals all have many interesting characteristics just waiting to be discovered. Each species of wildlife in Nunavut has its own special ways of surviving in the Arctic environment. We share this amazing and unique Arctic ecosystem with wildlife.

Ever since I was young, I have been learning about wildlife and I am still learning today. To me, it was fascinating to find out how wildlife was traditionally used by the Inuit, how animal behaviour changes through the seasons, how

ᐱᓪᓕᓐᐅᐸᐧᒡᓗ—ᓄᓇᐧᒪᑎᐳᑕᐅᒡᒡᐳᑕ ᐅᒪᔫᒡ
ᓴᐳᒪᓇᒪᐧᑯᐧᖅᑭᓇᒃᖅᑎᓇᒋ ᓄᓇᕐᒡ
ᐅᒪᖅᑲᐃᔪᓇᐃᒡᖅᑯᒻᔭᑯ ᓴᐳᓂᖅᑭᑎᓇᒋ.

ᑕᕝᐁᓂ ᐅᖅᑲᓕᒻᒪᒡᒥ, ᓄᓇᕐᒥ ᐅᒪᔫᓂ
ᐊᕐᑭᑯᑎᑦᖏᓇᖅ ᐃᑦᑎᓇᖅᑯᒡᑐᑕᐃᒡᖅᑐᒡᑕ, ᐃᑕᖃᕐᑕ
ᑕᒡᔪᒪᔭᑕ. ᑭᓇᓇᖅᑭᖅᓴᖅᐸᕐᑕ ᐅᖅᑲᓕᒻᒪᒡᒥᒃ
ᑖᒡᔭᒪᑲ ᑕᑦᐱᓐᑎᓇᒡᑯᒡᑐᑕ ᐱᖅᐸᓂᓇᖅᖏᖅᒃ
ᐃᑕᖃᓇᒡᑐ, ᐊᐱᓇᓅᑦᖅᑐᑕᐃᒡᓗ ᐃᖅᑲᓇᒥ
ᐊᒡᔪᓇᒡᖅᑎᓇᑕᐃᒡᓗ ᓄᓇᐃᒡᓇᖅ ᖃᐅᒪᓇᒡᖅᑎᓇᖅ
ᐅᒪᔭᑕᐃᒃ ᓄᓇᐃᒡᓇ ᖃᖓᕐᒃᒡᓇᒡᑐᒡᑕᒃ.
ᑕᕝᐁᑐᖅᑭ ᒪᑦᐱᓇᒡᓯᓇᒃ ᐅᖅᑲᓕᒻᖅᑎᓇᒡᒡᑐᑕᒃ,
ᑐᑭᔭᓇᒡᑭᖅᖁᑯᒃᒡᓇᒡᐊᖅᖅᒡᐳᑎᒡ ᑐᑭᕐᖁᖓᕐᒃᒡᓇᒡᑎᓇᒡᒡᓗ
ᓄᓇᕐᒡ ᐅᒪᔭᐳᓇᖅ ᖃᑕᒡᓗ ᐱᓪᓕᓐᐅᒻᓪᐧᑭᑦ
ᐃᑯᐧᓇᒃ ᐅᖃᓇᒡᒡᓗ.

environmental changes affect wildlife, and
most importantly, how we Nunavummiut
can protect wildlife so that it will remain in
Nunavut for future generations.

In this book, you will learn about
many wildlife species in Nunavut, some
of which you may have already seen. I
encourage you to share this book with
your friends and relatives, and to ask elders
and hunters in your community for their
knowledge about the wildlife near you. I
hope that through reading these pages,
you will gain a new appreciation and
understanding of Nunavut's wildlife.

ᓴᐃᒪᓐ ᐊᕙ
Simon Awa

ᓇᓂᖅᖃᐅᑉ ᐆᒪᔪᖕᒋᑦ
Animals of the Tundra

ᐊᕕᙵᖅ | Lemming

ᐊᕕᙵᐃᑦ ᒥᑭᓐᓂᖅᐹᖑᒍᑦ ᒥᖅᑯᓕᖕᓂᒃ ᐱᓱᒃᑎᓂᒃ ᐆᒪᔪᓂᑦ ᐅᑭᐅᖅᑕᖅᑐᒥ. ᖁᐃᓂᔫᒐᓗᐊᑦ ᐊᖕᒪᔪᒃᑯᑦ ᒥᑭᑦᑐᑯᓗᒃᑯᑦ ᐊᓂᒍᕈᓐᓇᖅᑐᑦ. ᐃᓚᖕᒋᑦ ᐅᑭᐅᒃᑯᑦ ᖃᑯᖅᓯᕙᒃᑐᑦ ᐱᖅᑲᑎᖕᒋᑦᑕᐅᖅ ᖃᖕᒐᓚᒦᖅ ᑲᔫᖕᒋᓐᓇᖅᐸᒃᑐᑦ. ᐊᐅᔭᒃᑯᑦ ᐊᕕᙵᐃᑦ ᑎᓯᓚᐅᓰᑦ ᓄᓇᒥᒃ ᐊᒡᒐᒃᕈᑎᒃ ᐅᑭᐅᖅᐸᑦ ᐊᑐᓖᖅᑕᒥᖕᓂᒃ. ᓄᖅᑲᖕᒐᕝᕕᖕᒥᖕᓂ ᐅᖅᑰᔾᔦᑎᒃᓴᒥᖕᓂᒃ ᐱᓰᑦ ᒪᑯᓂᖕᒐ ᐃᕚᑦ, ᓯᓗᓛᑦ, ᐊᒻᒪᓗ ᐅᒥᖕᒪᐃᑦ ᒥᖅᑯᖕᒋᓐᓂᒃ ᑲᑕᒐᕐᓂᑯᓂᒃ. ᐃᕿᕕᒃᑎᑐᑦ ᓴᓇᓯᒪᔪᓂᒃ ᐅᖅᑯᕕᒃᓴᒥᓂᒃ ᓴᓇᓯᒪᓰᑦ, ᐅᑭᐅᒃᑯᑦ ᑕᐃᑲᓂ ᑲᑎᙵᓪᓗᑎᒃ ᐅᖅᑰᑎᖅᑲᑦᑕᐅᑎᓰᑦ. ᐊᕕᙵᐃᑦ ᐃᓪᒥᖕᓄᑦ ᐆᖅᑲᑦᑕᐅᑎᓰᑦ ᐊᒻᒪ ᐋᓐᓂᖅᑲᑦᑕᐅᑎᕙᒃᕈᑎᒃ ᓂᑦᓚᐊᖅᑲᑦᑕᐅᑎᕙᒃᕈᑎᓪᓗ. ᑕᐃᔅᓯᒪᓂᑲᑦᓚᒃ ᐊᒥᖕᒋᑦ ᐊᑐᖅᑕᐅᕙᓚᐅᖅᑐᑦ ᒪᑦᑐᑎᒋᔭᐅᑦᑐᑎᒃ.

Lemmings are the smallest mammals in the High Arctic. They are chubby, but can squeeze through very small openings. There are two types—one type turns white in the winter and the other stays dark brown all year round. In the summer, lemmings dig tunnels into moss and tundra, to prepare for winter. They make warms nests with grasses, feathers, and muskox wool they find on the ground. Through the winter, they stay warm by huddling together in their nests. However, lemmings are also known to fight with each other. They will bite, punch, and squeal at their opponents. Lemming skins can be used as bandages to heal cuts and more serious wounds.

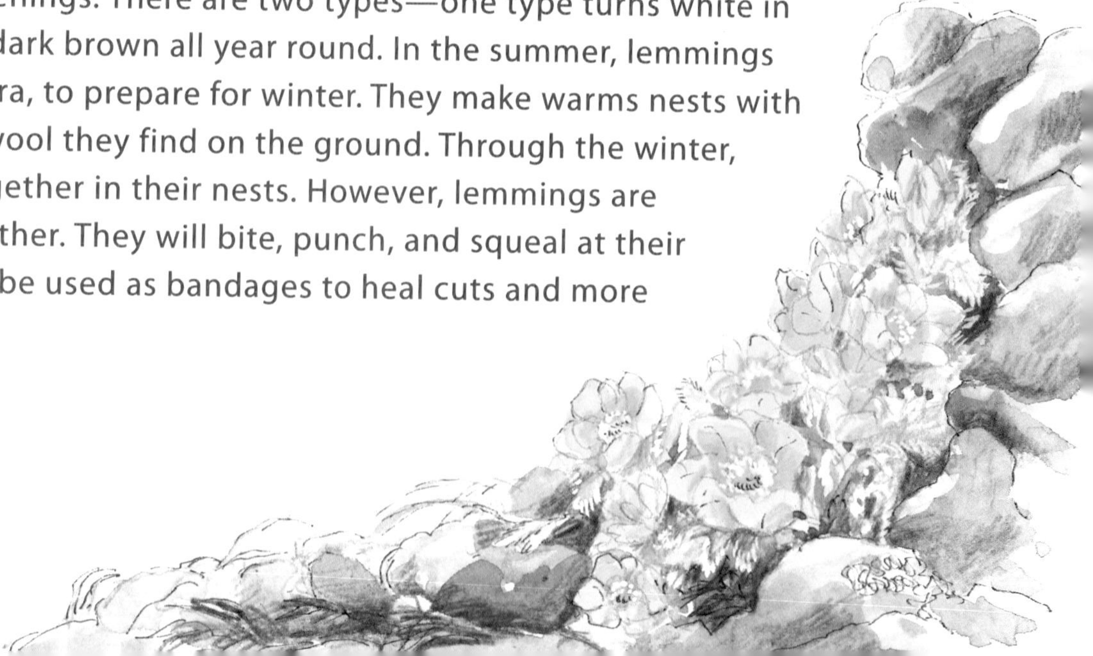

ᑐᒃᑐ ᐊᖅᑎᓂᖅᒃᕼᕝᖅᖅ | Barren-ground Caribou

ᑐᒃᑐᑦ ᐊᖅᑎᓂᖅᒃᕼᐃᑦ ᓄᓇᕗᒻᒥᖏᕆᐅᑕᖅᑐᑦ. ᐊᖅᒡᒍᒐᖕᒪᖅ ᓂᖅᒃᕼᖅᕝᐅᖅᒍᑎᒃ ᐱᓯᒃᑎᑦ.
ᓂᖅᒃᕼᒥᖅᓂᒃ ᓄᒡᒐᑎᕝᒡᖕᒥᒡ ᓂᖅᒃᕼᓂᒃ ᓄᓇᒍᑦ ᐊᒡᐊᓄᑦ ᐅᕝᕝᖅᑐᑦ. ᐅᑉᐅᕝᑯᑦ
ᓂᑎᐻᑐᐊᑕᕈᑦ ᐅᕝᖅᒃᑕ ᖅᒡᐊᐊᕕᐅᑎᖕᕝᖅᓂᒃ. ᐊᒻᒪᑕᕈᖅ ᐅᕝᐅᕝᑯᑦ ᐊᕈᑕᕼᖅᕝᒪᓂᖅᒻᒥᖅ
ᖅᓄᕕᑦ. ᐊᐅᕝᕝᑯᑦ ᐊᕈᑎᕈᐊᕝᖕᒪᓂᖅ ᐊᕈᒻᒥ ᓂᕝᒃᕼᕿᑎᐊᕝᑦ ᖅᕝᑐᑎᐊᓂᕝᒍ ᖅᐲᕝᒡᑐᖅ.
ᐻᒃᐊ ᐃᓇᖕᓂᒃ ᐊᑐᕼᒡᐅᕕᓇᖅᑐᑦ. ᐊᖃᓄᕝᕼᑎᐊᖅᐄᕝᔭᖕᖅᒪᑕ ᓴᕼᒍ ᐊᑎᑎ
ᖅᑕᑎᑦᑕᕕᖕᖅᑎᑦ. ᐅᕝᐊᖅᕼᕿᕝᐊᖅᑎᑎᒍ ᒻᖅᒡᐊᕝᑎᑦ ᐱᒻᖕᓂᖅᖅᐺᕝᒍᑦ ᐊᖅᓄᖅᖅᕼᕝᑎᑦ.
ᐅᕝᐅᑎᕼᐃᑦ ᑐᖅᑐᐊᕝᒪᑕ ᐊᒻᒪ ᐅᐱᖅᒪᖕᒃᑕ ᒻᖅᒡᒻᖅ ᕼᐃᕈᐊᕝᑐᓂ.

Barren-ground caribou live in many parts of Nunavut. They travel all year to find food, moving on when they have eaten most of it. Their main food source is lichen. To find lichen in the winter, they search for places where the wind has blown the snow from the land. In the summer, they search for patches of snow for relief from the heat and mosquitoes. Barren-ground caribou are essential to Inuit life. They are a major source of food and their skin is used to make clothing, such as parkas and wind pants. Caribou skin is best when the animal is caught in the autumn. In winter, barren-ground caribou fur is too thick, and in summer it is too thin.

ᑐᒃᑐ | Peary Caribou

ᑖᒃᑯᐊ ᑐᒃᑐᑦ ᒥᑭᓛᖑᔪᑦ ᑐᒃᑐᓕᒫᓂᑦ ᑭᓯᐊᓂ ᑕᑉᐹᓂ ᓂᒡᓚᓯᖕᓂᖅᐹᒦᑉᐸᒃᑐᑦ. ᑖᒃᑯᐊ ᖃᑦᑐᓈᑎᑐᑦ ᐱᐅᕆᒥᒃ ᐊᑎᖃᖅᑐᑦ. ᑕᐃᔅᓯᒥᖕᒐ ᐊᑎᖃᖅᑐᑦ ᖀᐳᑦ ᐱᐅᕆᒥᒃ ᑖᓐᓇ ᓯᕗᓪᓕᖅᐹᒥᒃ ᖃᑦᑐᓈᖑᑦᑐᓂ ᓄᓇᐅᑉ ᑲᔅᐹᖕᖓᓄᐊᕐᓂᑯᕕᓂᕐᒥᒃ. ᑖᒃᑯᐊ ᐅᓄᙱᑦᑐᑯᓘᑦᑐᑎᒃ ᐱᓱᓲᑦ ᐱᔾᔪᑎᒋᑦᑐᒍ ᓂᕿᒃᓴᖃᑦᑎᐊᙱᒻᒪᑕ ᑕᑉᐹᓂᐅᔭᖅ. ᓂᕿᒃᓴᒥᖕᓂᒃ ᓇᐃᒪᑦᑎᐊᖅᑐᐊᓘᖕᒪᑕ ᐊᐳᑎᐅᑉ ᐊᑖᓃᑦᑐᓂᒃ ᓇᐃᓲᑦ. ᓂᓇᓂᖅᐹᓇᕈᒃᑕᖕᒋᑦ ᐊᐅᐱᓚᑦᑐᙳᐊᑦ. ᐅᐱᕐᖔᒃᑯᑦ ᓂᓇᖅᑕᓗᐊᒍᑦ ᓱᒡᔪᖕᒋᑦ ᐊᐅᐸᔪᒃᓯᓲᑦ.

Peary caribou are the smallest caribou and live only on the High Arctic islands. They are named after Robert Peary, who is said to be the first European to have reached the North Pole. Peary caribou travel in very small groups because there is little food available in the High Arctic. Their strong sense of smell helps them find plants even when the land is covered by snow. In fact, they are so good at finding food that they can grow fat. Their favourite plant to eat is purple saxifrage. In early summer, they eat so much of it that their muzzles are stained purple!

ᓇᓕᓂᐊᖅ ᐅᑭᐅᖅᑕᖅᑐᒥ | Arctic Fox

ᐅᑭᐅᖅᑕᖅᑐᒥ ᓇᓕᓂᐊᑦ ᓂᕐᒧᑎᓂᑦ ᓯᓕᕐᒃᐊᒐᒥ ᒥᒥᓂᖅᖕᒡᐅᓯᑦ, ᒥᖅᑯᐊᑦ ᑐᖕᑭᓂᓗᓂᑦ ᐊᖕᑎᕐᓗᖅᑯᐱᕐᒥᑦ. ᒥᖅᑯᐊᑦ ᑐᖕᑎᓂᓗ ᐅᖅᑯᕆᕐᓇᑎᕐᖃᑐᖕᑕ ᐅᑭᐅᑦᑯᑦ. ᓇᓕᓂᐊᑦ ᐃᓕᖕᒥᑦ ᖃᑯᐅᑎᕐᒃᑐᑦ ᐃᓕᖕᒥᑦ ᑲᔨᒑᓗᑎᒃ ᐊᒪᒃ ᐃᓕᖕᒥᑦ ᓯᕐᓴᓂᐅᑎᓗᑎᒃ.

The Arctic fox is one of the smallest foxes in the world, but its thick fur makes it look bigger than it actually is. The fox's thick fur helps it survive the extreme cold. Arctic foxes are white, brown, or silver. The female fox gives birth to larger litters than any other mammal—from four to twenty pups at a time! The young foxes are born blind and deaf, and they have no teeth. Fox families live in dens, which they dig into hills and slopes where the ground is not frozen. They make many entrances and tunnels. Arctic foxes are poor hunters, so they often follow polar bears to eat their scraps. This habit has led them to some of the most remote Arctic islands.

ᖃᕝᕕᐅᔨᕐᔪᒃ | Wolverine

ᖃᕝᕕᐅᔨᕐᔮᑦ ᓇᐃᑦᑐᖃᕐᐸᐅᒐᔾᑐᑎᒃ ᓴᓐᑎᒐᑎᒃ ᓂᕐᖑᖔᓴᖅᒃᔪᐳᖅᐸᑐᒋᑦ. ᖁᓂᖅᐳᖃᒃᑲᐅᑦᒎᑎᒎᓗ
ᓴᓐᑎᕐᕙᔪᖮᒎᑎᒃ ᒥᒃᑐᑐᓪᒎᕝᓛᑦ. ᒡᕐᕗᐊ ᒥᒃᑐᒔᓗᒎᕝᓛᑦ ᑐᒡᑐᒥᖮ ᑐᒐᑦᑎᕐᕐᓇᖅᒋᑦ, ᑭᔨᐊᓂ
ᓂᖅᐅᓂᒐᓂᖮ (ᓂᓯᕐᐅᓂᒐᓂᖮ) ᑐᖮᑐᓂᖮ ᐊᒪᖅᒀᓂᒐ (ᐊᒪᔨᖓᓂ) ᓇᐢᓄᓂᖮᒎ (ᓇᓄᖮᓂᒎ).
ᖃᕝᕕᐅᔨᕐᕙᑦ ᐃᔪᓕᖮᕐᕐᖮ ᐃᓄᐃᑦ ᐊᒡᒪᖮᕐᑎᑐᖮ ᑕᒪᐃᐊᖮᕝᖮᖮ ᒥᕐᖮᓂᖅᕐᔃᖮᖮᐊᖮᐳᖮᒎᑎᖮ
ᓴᓐᑎᕐᕙᔪᖮᒎᑎᖮ. ᐅᕐᕐᖮᓂᖮ ᐱᔨᐊᕐᖮᖮᖅᒎᑦ ᖮᖮᖓᐅᖮ ᐅᕐᕐᖮᖮᓂᖮ ᐱᖮᖮᔮᖮᐊᒐᖮᒎ
ᓂᑕᒎᑎᖮ. ᖃᕝᕕᐅᔨᕐᕙᑦ ᑐᖮᑐᓂᖮ ᑕᖮᕐᐊᕐᓂᖮ ᒪᓂᖮᕝᖮᔃᑦ ᑕᖮᑲᐅᕙᖮᑎᖮ. ᐊᖮᐊᖮᑐᐊᖮ
ᐃᖮᐊᐃᖮ ᓄᐊᖮᖅᖮᕝᖮᔃᑦ ᐃᐄᖮᐊᖮᖓᖮᖓ, ᐊᖮᖮᖮᐊᖮᖮᖮᐅᖮᖮᖮᔃᐊᖮᖮᖮᖮᖮᐅᕙᖮᔃᑦ
ᓄᐊᖮᖮᖮᖮᖮᖮ. ᖃᕝᕕᐅᔨᕐᕙᑦ ᓄᐊᖮᖮᖮᐊᕑᐅᓂᖮᕝᖮᔃᒎᖮ ᐳᐊᖮᖮᐊᕑᐅᖮᒎᑎᖮᒎ
ᖮᓂᖮᖮᖮᖮᖮᖮ.

Wolverines are short, stout scavengers. They are curious and bold. They have great strength for their size. They are strong enough to kill caribou, but they prefer to eat caribou carcasses left behind by wolves and bears. The wolverine's paws are like hands, but are smaller and very strong. They can remove rocks from food caches to get the meat inside. Wolverines follow caribou herds and are able to travel far without tiring. Adult female wolverines stay in the area where they were born, but adult males travel far to find new territories. Wolverine fur is one of the best materials for trimming parkas and mittens because it does not gather frost.

ᑕᕆᐅᑉ ᓯᑯᓪᓖᓗ ᐅᒪᔪᖏᑦ

Animals of the Sea and Ice

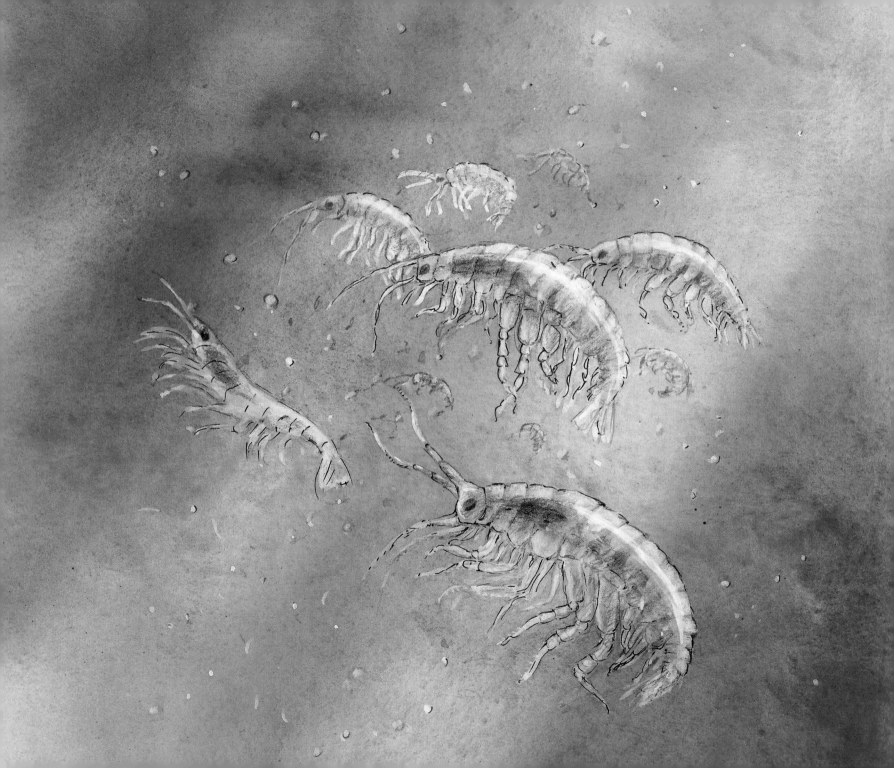

Ꮮᵘᒐᐃᶜ | Amphipods

Ꮮᵘᒐᐃᶜ ᒥᖃᑐᔭᶜ ᖃᖃᖃᖰᐳᶜ Ꮮᵘᒐᖃᐸᖃᐱᑐᔭᶜ. ᓲᕝᑯᐊ ᐱᏞᔪᖁᒐᕝᶜ 2ᒥᕝᕙᒥᒐᶜ 50ᒥᕙᕙᒥᒐᖵ ᑕᏞᓂᖃᕝᒐᕝᔾᶜ. ᐊᔾᐱᖁᖰᒐᑐᖴ Ꮮᵘᒐᖰᑕᖃᐸᔪᔪᐳᖃ. ᐃᖖᖨᒐᶜ ᔪᕝᕕᒥᔪᔨᔭᶜᑐᖴ, ᐃᖖᖨᒐᶜ ᔪᕝᑯᶜ ᐊᐱᖖᖰᖁᔾᔪᔭᶜᑐᖴ, ᐃᖖᖰᒐᶜ ᑕᔾᖃᓂ, ᖕᒥᓕᓂᔪ. Ꮮᵘᒐᐃᶜ ᐃᖖᖰᖃᖃᖁᐳᔪᖖᒐᑐᶜ Ꮮᔾᐊᓂ ᓂᖃᖓᔨᒐᖖᖰᓂᖃ ᐱᓇᕝᔪᖖᒐᑐᑎᐊᖃᑐᶜ. ᓂᖰᖃᖁᑐᶜ ᓂᕝᒐᑎᓂᖃ ᐃᒥᓂ ᑐᕝᖕᓂᖕᓂᖃ. ᑕᒪᐃᔪᒪᒐᶜ ᑕᓄᐳᒐᖃ ᐃᒥᕝᖃᖃ ᔭᒐᒪᒐᑎᑎᖖᖀᔾᖃᖰᐳᖃᶜ. ᖁᖄᓂ ᓂᖦᖃᔾᖃᑐᓂ ᐊᑐᖰᔾᐳᖃᶜ ᐃᒥᕝᒐᐳᑕᖖᖀᶜ ᓂᖰᖃᖁᑐᶜ ᒪᑯᖄᖖᖁᕝᶜ, ᐃᖃᑐᖃ, ᖏᖰᒥᐊᖃᓂᶜ ᐃᒥᕝᒐᐳᑕᕝᖁᖃᖃᶜ, ᖃᑎᖓᐊᖄᓂᕝᖁᖃᶜ ᐊᖐᒐᔪ ᐊᕝᖄᕝᖁᖃᶜ.

Amphipods are tiny shellfish that look like small shrimp. They grow from two to fifty millimetres long. They breathe through gills. Most amphipods live in holes in the sea ice or under pack ice. Amphipods are poor swimmers, but very good scavengers. They eat animals that have died in the water. This helps keep the ocean clean. Amphipods are important in the Arctic ecosystem because they are food for many other animals, such as fish, seabirds, and young seals.

ᐃᖃᓗᒃ ᑕᕆᐅᕐᒥᐅᑕᖅ | Arctic Char

ᑕᕆᐅᕐᒥᐅᑕᐃᑦ ᐃᖃᓗᐃᑦ ᓂᓪᓚᓱᒃᑐᕐᒥᐅᑕᐅᓂᖅᐹᖑᕗᑦ ᐃᖃᓘᖃᑎᓕᒫᒥᖕᓂᑦ. ᑕᖅᓴᖏᑦ ᐃᓚᖓ ᑲᔫᑦᑐᓂ, ᐃᓚᖓ ᖁᖅᓱᖅᑐᖅ, ᐃᓚᖓ, ᖁᖅᓱᒃᑲᓇᒃᑐᖅ, ᐃᓚᖓ ᐊᐅᐸᔪᒃᑐᖅ ᐊᐅᐸᖅᑐᕐᓘᓐᓃᑦ. ᒪᕐᕈᐃᓂᒃ ᐃᖃᓗᑦᓚᑖᓂᒃ ᐱᑕᖃᔫᖑᕗᖅ ᓄᓇᕗᒻᒥ ᐃᕕᓵᕈᐃᑦᓗ ᑕᕆᐅᕐᒥᐅᑕᐃᑦᓗ. ᐃᕕᓵᕈᐃᑦ ᐊᕐᕌᒍᓕᒫᖅ ᑕᓯᕐᒦᓰᑦ ᑕᕆᐅᕐᒥᐅᑕᐃᑦ ᑕᕆᐅᒨᖅᓯᒪᓰᑦ ᐊᒻᒪ ᑕᓯᕐᒧᑦ ᐅᑎᒃᑲᓐᓂᖅᖢᑎᒃ. ᑕᕆᐅᕐᒥᐅᑕᐃᑦ ᑭᖑᖕᓂᒃ ᓂᕆᔫᖑᕗᑦ. ᐊᒻᒪ ᐆᒐᕐᓂᒃ ᓂᕆᔫᖑᒋᑦᓗᑎᒃ ᑕᕆᐅᕐᒥᐅᑕᐃᑦ ᐊᐅᔭᒃᑯᑦ ᑕᕆᐅᕐᒦᑉᐸᒃᑐᑦ ᓂᕆᑦᑎᐊᑲᑕᒃᖢᑎᒃ ᖁᐃᒃᑎᖢᑎᒃ. ᐅᑭᐊᒃᓵᖑᓕᕌᖓᑦ ᑕᓯᕐᒧᑦ ᑰᒃᑯᑦ ᐅᑎᖅᐸᒃᖢᑎᒃ. ᑕᕆᐅᕐᒥᐅᑕᐃᑦ ᒪᒪᕐᓂᖅᐹᖑᕗᑦ ᐊᐅᔭᒃᑯᑦ. ᑕᐃᔅᓱᒪᓂᒃᑲᓂᖅ ᐃᖃᓘᑉ ᐊᒥᕋᖏᑦ ᐴᓚᐊᕆᔭᐅᕙᓚᐅᖅᑐᑦ ᓴᓇᕐᕈᑎᓄᑦ. ᓂᐊᖁᖓ ᓴᐅᓂᖏᑦᓗ ᐲᖅᑕᐅᑦᓗᑎᒃ, ᐊᒥᕋᖓ ᐸᓂᖅᓱᐊᕆᔭᐅᑦᓗᓂ. ᐊᕐᕕᐊᕐᒥᐅᓂᑦ ᐊᕐᑭᐊᒧᐊᑕ (ᓈᖓᑕ) ᐅᖅᓱᖏᑦ ᖁᓪᓕᕐᒧᑦ ᐅᖅᓱᕆᔭᐅᕙᓚᐅᖅᑐᑦ.

Arctic char live farther north than any other freshwater fish. They can be brown, yellow, gold, orange, or red. There are two types of char in Nunavut—landlocked char and sea-run char. Landlocked char stay in lakes all year round while sea-run char travel to the sea for part of the year. Sea-run char are bigger than landlocked char. Char love to eat amphipods. They also eat tiny cod fish and anything else they can catch. Sea-run char spend the summer in the ocean eating and growing fat. By late summer, they swim back to the rivers and lakes. The most delicious char to eat are sea-run char caught in late June. In the past, char skins were made into sacks to carry tools. The head of the char was cut off, the meat and bones were removed, and then the skin was left to dry. Around Arviat, people also used the stomach fat of char as fuel for their qulliq (traditional lamp).

ᐅᒡᔪᒃ | Bearded Seal

ᐅᒡᔪᐃᑦ ᖃᑦᑐᓈᑎᑐᑦ ᑕᐃᔭᐅᓲᖕᒪᑕ ᐅᒥᓂᖕᓂᒃ ᑖᒃᑯᐊ ᑕᐃᒪᓐᓇ ᐊᑎᖃᖅᑎᑕᐅᕗᑦ ᖃᓂᖓ ᐊᕿᑖ ᒥᖅᑯᖃᕐᓂᖓᓄᑦ ᐅᒥᐅᖅᑰᔨᑦᑐᑎᒃ. ᐅᒥᖏᑦ ᐃᒃᐱᖕᓂᐊᑦᑎᐊᕐᒪᑕ ᓂᕿᒃᓴᒥᖕᓂᒃ ᐃᒪᐅᑉ ᐃᖅᑲᖓᓂᑦ ᐱᓲᑦ. ᑕᓕᕈᕐᒥᖕᓄᑦ ᓂᕿᒃᓴᒥᖕᓂᒃ ᐱᓲᑦ. ᒪᑯᓂᖓ ᑭᖑᒃᐸᖕᓂᒃ, ᐊᒻᒨᒪᔪᑦ ᐊᒻᒪ ᐊᓯᖏᓐᓂᒃ ᑭᓯᑐᐃᓐᓇᑦᑎᐊᓂᒃ ᐊᒻᒪ ᓇᓂᔭᒥᖕᓂᒃ ᓂᕆᕙᒃᑐᑦ. ᐅᒡᔪᐃᑦ ᐅᑭᐅᓚᒦᖅ ᐃᒦᓂᓲᑦ. ᐅᖅᓱᖃᕐᒪᑕ ᐃᔾᔪᔪᒥᒃ ᑕᐃᒪᓐᓇ ᐅᖅᑰᔪᓐᓇᖅᐳᑦ ᐃᒦᓂ. ᐅᒡᔪᐃᑦ ᐃᒦᓂ ᐃᖕᒋᕐᕿᒃᑲᐅᕗᑦ. ᐃᓅᓵᖅᑐᑎᒃ ᐃᒃᑲᕐᖃᐃᑦ ᖃᔅᓲᓇᐃᑦ ᐃᓅᓯᒪᓕᖅᑐᑎᒃ ᐃᖕᒋᕐᕿᔪᓐᓇᖅᓯᑲᐅᑎᒋᕙᒃᑐᑦ. ᐅᒡᔪᐃᑦ ᕿᓯᖕᒋᑦ ᓯᖁᔾᖖᒋᑐᐊᓗᐃᑦ ᑖᒃᑯᐊ ᐊᒃᓗᓈᑕᐊᖑᓰᑦ ᐊᑕᒃᓴᑕᐊᖑᑦᑐᑎᒃ, ᕿᒻᒥᓄᑦ ᐃᐱᐅᑕᓇᔅᓴᐅᑦᑐᑎᒃ ᐊᓄᒋᔅᓴᐅᑦᑐᑎᒡᓗ ᐊᒻᒪ ᑲᒥᖕᓄᑦ ᐊᑐᖕᖓᒋᔅᓴᐅᕙᒃᑐᑎᒃ.

The bearded seal is named for the many whiskers around its mouth, which resembles a beard. Their whiskers help them feel prey in the water. Bearded seal eat mostly shrimp, clams, and whelks from the sea bottom, but they will eat almost anything else they find. They use their large, square flippers to dig up food. Bearded seals spend most of their time in the water. A thick layer of fat under their skin keeps them warm. Bearded seals are good swimmers. The babies can swim just a few hours after they are born! The skin of bearded seals is very strong, so it is used to make ropes, harpoon lines, dog harnesses, and soles for boots. The intestines of bearded seals can also be stretched and dried to make windows for sod houses.

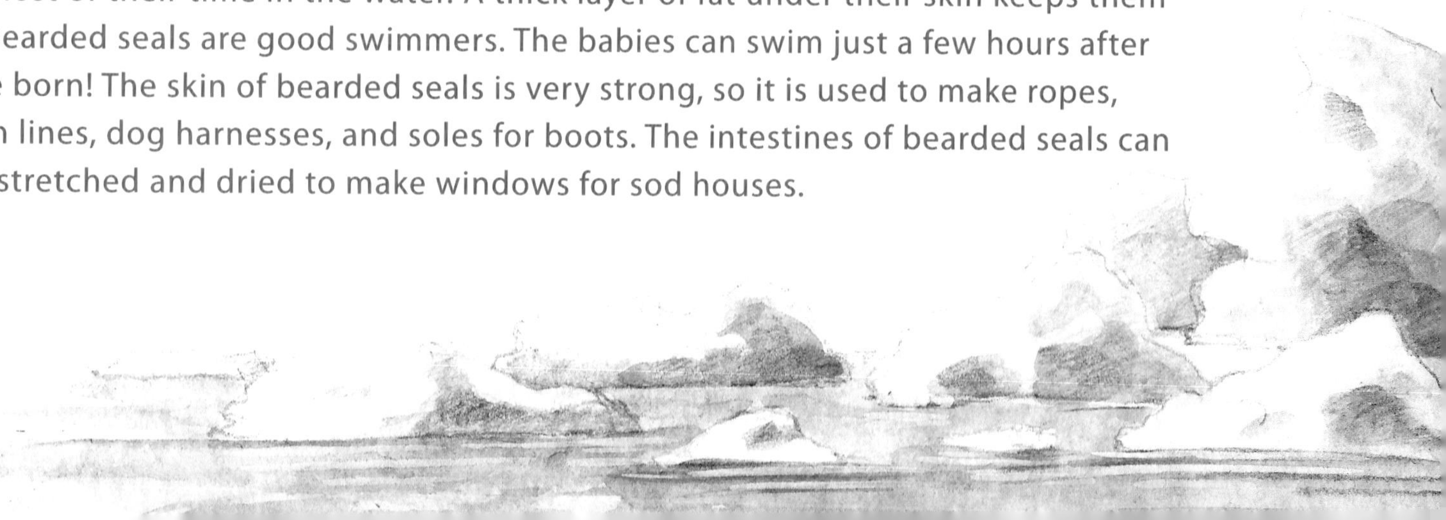

ᖃᐸᓗᒡᒥᐅ | Beluga

ᖅᑲᐅᑦᓗᑕᖅ ᖅᑲᓗᒐᐅᐊᑦ ᑲᑎᕛᓯᕙᒃᑐᑦ ᖅᕐᔭᐊᓇᐅᑦᓄᑉ ᒫᓂ ᑦᑕᒐᓂᑦ ᖅᑐᓂᒥᑦ ᑖᒪᐤᓇ ᐅᓄᖅᑎᕐᕙᒃᑐᑦ. ᔭᓴᐅᕝ ᖅᑲᓄᐃᕝᕝᑦᑕᐊᓯᕐᒪᒫᓯᑐ ᑖᒪᐊᒻᕙᖅ. ᐊᖅᑲᐅᒪᕐᓯᖏᑦ 20 ᒥᓂᑦᕈᓂᒃ ᐊᓇᖅᖁᑕᐅᖖᒦᓇᓯᑐᑉ. ᖅᑲᓗᒐᐅᐊᑦ ᐃᓇᕙᒃᐳᑦ ᐊᐅᐸᖅᓄᑉ ᑲᕐᓄᑎᖖᒡᐄᑦ. ᐃᓇᕐᓯᓴᖅᓯᑐᑉ ᑕᖅᓴᖖᒪ ᑕᖅᓴᐅᒃᑲᓂᖕᕙᒃᐳᑦ ᐊᕐᓴᐊᓗᒃ ᐊᖕᐅᓇᑦᕙᕐᒪ ᖅᑲᐅᑐᖅᓱᕙᒃᑐᑉ. ᖅᑲᓗᒐᐅᐊᑦ ᐃᓇᕐᔾᕌᒥᕐᒥ ᐊᑦᕉᔪᐊᓄᑉ ᒪᔭᕋᓄᑉ ᐊᕐᑲᒥᖕᕙᒐᐤᑦ. ᖅᑲᓗᒐᐅᐊᑦ ᐊᑎᖅᒃᑎᑕᐅᖖᒍᐊᕐᔾᒐᕐᑦᑦ "ᑕᓄᐅᒥ ᑎᖕᒡᕙᑦ" ᐃᒫᓂ ᐅᐊᖖᕐᕠᖅᓄᑉ ᐊᕐᔾᕐᓄᓂᒃᓄ ᓂᑦᑦᐊᕐᔾᐅᓄᐤᕈᓇᒥᑦᓄᑉ ᐊᑎᖅᖅᑎᑕᐅᕙᒃᐳᑦ. ᖅᑲᓗᒐᐅᐊᑦ ᐊᕐᔪᓇᕐᒃᑕᐅᕙᒃᐳᑦ ᒫᒃᑕᐊᖖᒪᓄᑉ ᐊᐅᔪᑦ ᐱᐅᕐᔾᒥᑉ ᐊᕐᔾᕐᓄᓂᒃᓄ ᐃᑲᕐᔾᑕᖅᑦᓄᖕᑦᓂᒃ ᐱᖅᖁᒫᑦ. ᐊᒻᒪᑦᑕᐅᖅ ᐅᖅᔾᕐᖖ ᖅᑯᓪᓕᐊᔾᑦ ᐅᖅᖅᓯᑎᕈᐅᕙᒃᑦᓄᓂ.

Beluga whales are pink or brown when they are born. In their first weeks of life, they turn dark grey, and then white as they grow into adults. Beluga babies stay with their mothers for at least two years. Belugas live in small pods of about five to ten whales. They hunt together and travel with the seasons. They can swim underwater for twenty minutes without going to the surface for air. Belugas have been nicknamed the "canaries of the sea" because of the whistles, groans, clicks, and other noises that they make. Belugas are hunted for their skin, known as maktaaq, which is rich in vitamin C and other nutrients. Beluga fat is also used as fuel for the qulliq.

ᐊᕐᕕᖅ | Bowhead Whale

ᐊᕐᕕᑦ ᐊᖑᑎᒋᔪᖅᑲᑕᐅᕗᑦ ᓯᓛᕐᔪᐊᕐᒥ. ᓇᐊᕐᑯᖅᑯᖅᑐᑦᑐᓄᒃ, ᓱᒡᒥᒃ ᔅᕐᒃᔅᔅᑎᑎᕐᑫᒃᑕᒣᔅᒃ ᐃᒪᐅᐸᑦ ᖄᙱᒪᐊᕙᑎᐊᕐᑕᐅᕐᔅᐃᒥᒃ. ᐊᕐᕙᖦᔪᑦᑐᖏᒃ ᖅᒃᓯᖏᔅ, ᐊᕠᐃᔅᖅᖅᐅᑕᓲᓯᓂᖅᒪᑕᖅᐸᑯᑐ ᑕᑦᔪᒐᔅ ᑕᓚᔪᕐᒥᑎᑐᓘ ᓴᖅᐱᖅᑎᑐᓘᕐ. ᐊᕐᕕᑦ ᐊᑯᓇᒻᒪᑎᐊᒍᒃ ᐃᖑᔅᔅᔪᖏᑦ ᑖᒃᐊᔪᑦ ᐃᒪᕐᒪᐅᑕᓂ ᐃᖑᔅᔅᔅᓂᖅᐸᖦᔅᔅᑰᒃᑐᖓᖅᒃᒪᒃᑐᖅ ᐊᕐᕠᒍᓄᑦ 200ᓂᑦ ᐃᖑᕐᖦᖅᑐᑦ. ᐃᓄᖦᓂᑦᓗ ᐊᕐᔅᖦᖏᑦᓗ ᑖᒃᒐᖅᖑᔪᐊᕐ ᐱᓇᔅᖅᑕᐅᕐᖅᔅᑦ. ᑖᒃᐊ ᑲᔅᐱᐊᕐᑕᕐᔅᔅᓕᒥᒃ ᐃᒪᕐᔨᒃ ᖅᐲᔅᖦᕐᑦ. ᐃᓄᖦᓂᑦ ᓂᖅᐱᕐᔅᐅᔦᓚᑐᖅᒃᑐ ᐊᒻᒥᓗ ᓴᕇᐅᖏᕐᑦ ᐃᔅᓘᒥᖦᓂᑦ ᖅᖃᓕᔅᖦᐅᖅᕐᔅᓄᑦᒃ ᐊᒻᒥᓗ ᓴᓇᕐᖅᐱᑎᐊᕐᔅᖦᕐᔅᓄᑦᒃ. ᐊᕐᕕᑦ ᐅᖅᔅᔅᖏᑦ ᔅᖅᐸᓚᕐᔅᔅᓲᑎᖅᐅᖅᔅᐲᖅᑎᐊᕐᐱᐅᕗᔅᖅ.

Bowhead whales are one of the largest whales in the world. They have huge heads, which they use to break sea ice when they need to reach the surface. Young bowhead whales are black, but white marks show up on their chin, flukes, and tail as they age. Bowhead whales may be the longest living mammal in the world—they are known to live over 200 years. Humans and killer whales are the only predators of these giant whales. When bowheads are threatened, they hide under the sea ice. They are slow swimmers.

ᐱᒃ ᑰᓕᑉ°ᐱ
Neil Christopher

ᒎᐅᐟ ᕿᓕᐳᕐᑎ
Louise Flaherty

ᓕᐊ ᐅᑕᒃ
Leah Otak

ᖱᒥ ᑲᕌᖅ
Romi Caron

ᑲᑖᓄᖅ ᒪᒃᑖᓕᒃ
Stephanie McDonald

ᓯᒪᓐ ᐊᕙ
Simon Awa

ᐋᓇ ᓯᒡᓕᒃ
Anna Ziegler

ᐊᐅᓚᑦᑎᔨᓄᑦ | Contributors

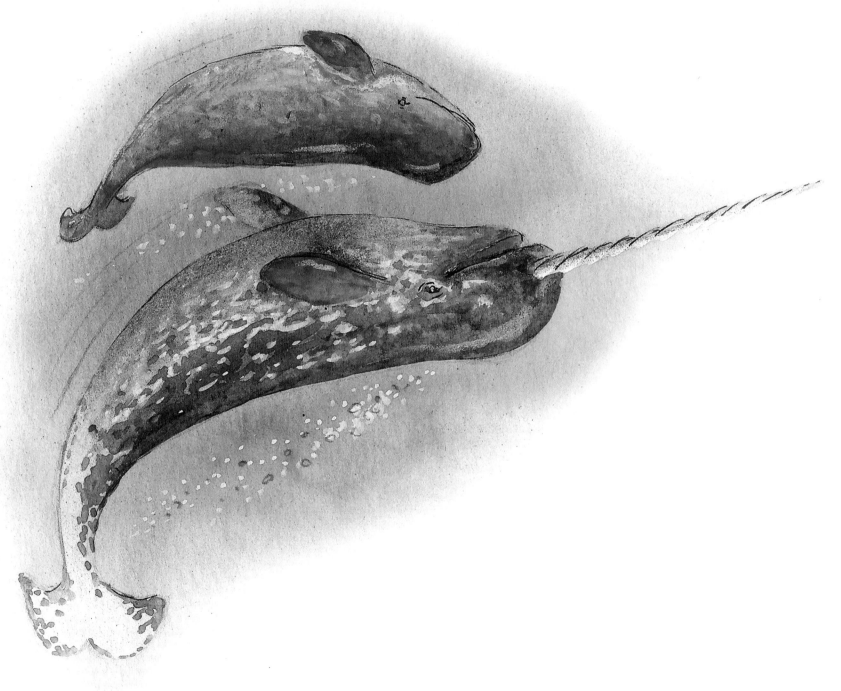